The Year of What Now

The Year of What Now

POEMS .

Brian
Russell

Graywolf Press

This publication is made possible, in part, by the voters of Minnesota through a Minnesota State Arts Board Operating Support grant, thanks to a legislative appropriation from the arts and cultural heritage fund, and through a grant from the National Endowment for the Arts. Significant support has also been provided by Target, the McKnight Foundation, Amazon.com, and other generous contributions from foundations, corporations, and individuals. To these organizations and individuals we offer our heartfelt thanks.

Published by Graywolf Press
250 Third Avenue North, Suite 600
Minneapolis, Minnesota 55401

www.graywolfpress.org

Published in the United States of America

ISBN 978-1-55597-648-4

2 4 6 8 9 7 5 3 1
First Graywolf Printing, 2013

Library of Congress Control Number: 2013931487

Cover design: Kyle G. Hunter

Cover photo: Colourbox

for Stephanie

Contents

The
Rhythm
of the
Empire

In the
Dark
and
Wait

Back
to
You

Introduction

The Year of What Now is not a book of poems about cancer. It's not a book that wears its heart on its sleeve. It doesn't parade the autobiographical in your face, though the conventions seem at first to be autobiography. It's not a cry *in extremis, de profundis,* etc. It's more casual, more canny, more casually well-made, more philosophically oriented, though without the pretentiousness of a smart-sounding vocabulary.

Because this is an art that knows its own mind, wonderfully independent of current period styles, the poems don't give a damn about toeing the line of some aesthetic camp or other: *fragmentation good, closure bad;* or *closure good, indeterminacy bad.* Instead, the poems are devoted to finding a way to speak intelligently, and movingly, and with an attractive and well-founded skepticism, about a "you" who is sick, who is anything but resigned or noble, and may, in fact, be a projection of the poet's imagination, though a fully embodied one, more embodied than a "real" person might be. Could it be that the wife who is dying in these poems doesn't really exist? And if she doesn't exist, why is the poet so interested in engineering her shock in discovering that she's ill, her time spent in a hospital trying to be cured, and her eventual, if equivocal, recovery?

I frame this book in this way so that unwary readers won't simply skate along on the surface of the story of a woman's illness. I want to forestall the simple-minded response that the reader has to cut the poet slack because his wife is dying or has almost died. Nobody should read this book as an underhanded attempt to play on our sympathies, to wring out a handkerchief, or to disarm our critical faculties because, well, it just wouldn't be nice to doubt the poet's sincerity.

In fact, it seems to me that this book's speaker is a kind of hologram of a mind up against the limits of science, medical technology, the clinic as a model of the world, and the endless routine of diagnostic tests that open out to philosophical conundrums that are both shatteringly personal and meant to remain detached. The hospital with its routine of death or cure, or limbo between the two, is drenched with a kind of alienating otherness. As Rimbaud might have said of the body and its relation to the X-ray, or to the experience of watching "them stick the needle in your back," *je est un autre*. Not I *am* an other. But I *is* an other: as if the mind, in trying to escape the body's pain, had tried to reduce itself to a mere projection of grammar.

But the body isn't so easy to escape: nobody having a needle stuck in their back is going to tell you that all they're feeling is the self/language dichotomy. Pain is always personal, pain always says *I am*—and when a person is in pain, no puritanical bromides about the unworthy solipsisms of "I" will make you feel it any less. In fact, in order to hang onto who you are, you need to assert your personal identity, even as it's being stripped from you—a paradox "Tepid" so beautifully illustrates.

> I still can't bring myself to watch
> them stick the needle in your back   you put up little
> resistance   a switch
> is flipped   you become the tortured
> trunk of a wind ravaged tree   rigid above an obsidian
> swamp of pain   mosquitoes linger
> at the surface   you feel them all over
> little diligent syringes drawing blood until
> they decide enough is
> enough   the muscles constrict   hard
> as bark   ashen limbs host a murder of birds
> prematurely dressed for mourning   your mouth a hollow

O   inside the restless snake
uncoils in the humidity of its new fangled hunger

The poet-snake inside the wife's mouth turns out in "Everything Every Time" to be another aspect of the speaker's hunger for reassurance against death—her death, and then his own. But as the poem plays out, all the identities in the room become algorithms of who is dying and who is observing, who is helping the dying and who is waiting their turn to die.

in a different version of this I'm the one
sitting up in bed while the nurse says
deep breaths   listens to my lungs through
the cold antenna of her stethoscope   you're the one
sitting in a chair in the corner
with a half hearted smile plastered to your face

in a different version of this
we're both in bed   hunched over
while two nurses   sisters actually   listen
to our lungs   your husband and my wife
sit in the corners of the room
both of them completely useless

in a different version of this I'm in a chair
in the corner while my sister sits up
in bed   you're the nurse who listens
to my sister breathing   you glance at me for
an instant and return my uncertain smile

The speaker breaks out of these claustrophobic ruminations in a poem like "Awash"—a restless determination to break down the boundaries between the cloistered room and the wider world, in which the wife's potential death becomes an invitation to remake the world:

the unthinkable prospect
of a world in which I am left
to my own devices

which are few and as soon
as the batteries die useless
first order of business

I draw a map in the sand
mark where I stand as the capital
of civilization   within me the
detailed blueprints of the pyramids
and the concept of zero
beyond me the finite frontier

the many miles of undeveloped
shoreline with spectacular views of a
sea filled with intricately depicted
monsters   I have a lot to do before

I introduce the new world
to art and astronomy and industry
medicine and technology
ethics politics democracy

by a show of hands we shall elect
which tree to burn in the first fire

What I admire in this poem is how clearly, cleanly written it is (all of Russell's poems are wonderfully lucid), while retaining what Ezra Pound said was William Carlos Williams's saving grace: opacity. The opacity in "Awash" isn't due to fragmentation, or lots of murky abstractions masquerading as profundities. It's not the result of a stylistic tic, Sensibility Unleashed, or the resort to a playbook of quirky poetic moves. No, it's much subtler than that, a matter of managing vocal tones with just the right degree of emphasis. The opacity here results from the tonal dissonance between the concluding couplet's mockery of the poet's own grandiosity, even as he underlines the irony that to make one world is to destroy another. This habit of mind pervades the collection, and is one of the most impressive aspects of Russell's work.

This book seems to me to represent a way forward for other young poets in its wide engagement with the world, in its unabashed embrace of the personal, and its equally galvanizing skepticism about the limits of subjective speech. At its deepest level, it embodies the desire to establish true sequences of pain from the cellular level to the most abstract operations of culture, technology, and possible worlds of the spirit.

Tom Sleigh
October 2012

The Year of What Now

It's a
Strange
City

We Remain This Way

your hands were stained the urgent shade
of blood   when I found you
you held them out to me as if holding a gift
as if they contained something of more
substance   something you wanted
me to take   but I didn't want this   I didn't know
what to do with it   we remained that way
for centuries   two useless statues commemorating
an event that no one remembers   even now
it's unclear which of us asked   what happened

In the Event

a cramped room at the end
of the hall   at the end
of the first day

it's clear you don't
understand the question

your eyes shot red with
vessels and endless
corridors   when I don't know
what to say I make a joke

if you were a vegetable
what kind of vegetable
do you want to be

you're not laughing

but you get it   you say
pull the plug I guess

what was I thinking
this is serious god
damn it   when you take
my hand I think   I don't care
what you say
I'm going to save you

Waiting for Radiation

a procession of wheelchairs await
admittance to radiation   ahead of you

a skinny kid in glasses
big enough to belong to the man
he might become

what are you in for
you ask him   the boy's father looks at you
then me   his face a shifting landscape of shock
and anger   the boy only shrugs
says I don't know   maybe cancer
what about you

you tell him what you know

you don't know

that's how it happens   fragile
bonds form   you and this boy the unstable
center the father and I spin circles around

this thing takes forever
the father says   I nod   I know
are they getting paid by the hour or what

a sound passes for a laugh
it's pretty clear
neither of us is holding it together

On Airs Waters and Places

it's a strange city   the commerce
of youth and the
commerce of death   merchants
of both talk the language
of the deal   under the table
the rug is pulled out from
under everyone   the most basic
human needs   from these we proceed
to investigate
everything else

a large crowd gathers
around a small stall   but what is
that man selling   can you tell

the crowd erupts
in applause   the sudden thunder of the
empty handed

The Year of What Now

I ask your doctor
of infectious disease if she's
read Williams   he cured
sick babies I tell her and
begin describing spring
and all   she's looking at the wall
now the floor   now your chart
now the door   never
heard of him she says
but I can't stop explaining
how important this is
I need to know your doctor
believes in the tenacity of nature
to endure   I'm past his heart
attack   his strokes   and now as if
etching the tombstone myself   I find
I can't remember the date
he died or even
the year   of what now
are we the pure products   and what
does that even mean   pure   isn't it
obvious   we are each our own culture
alive with the virus that's waiting
to unmake us

For Good

just after the last
shift change for the night   after visiting
hours end   all the concerned citizens
kiss the fevered foreheads of the damned
and don't waste a minute getting back
to their cars and their normal
lives   that's when the ambient noise of this
place separates into discernible tones
that rise to the surface of consciousness   splintered
bits of a sunken ship   first the sporadic
chirps from the legion of machines that keeps
everyone alive   somewhere down the hall a man
coughs violently then abruptly
stops   two new nurses safe at their station
speak in muffled tones   one is convinced
that someone named Eric is going to leave her
for good this time   the other tries to be
reassuring   like she learned   they're too
wrapped up in their own devotion to
the magic to notice the other
already knows the secret   quietly they return
to their work   a rustling of papers   the steady
clack of keys   heels down a long empty hallway

Again and Again

all week on the pullout couch
in the den your father talks in his sleep
to his wife   your mother   god rest
her soul in the fertile ground   a thousand miles
away she gives herself now
as she did to you to the endless
groves of orange trees   she feeds
them well   watches
them grow until they tower over her as
children do   they produce an honest fruit
like she taught them to

your father hides
in the shadows of the house   the spaces of
his grief   he's afraid he's
been here before   he shudders   he steps through

the sliding doors into the hospital's frigid imperative
when he looks at you he sees her too

Meanwhile Here on Earth

everyone we know is so
sorry to hear about you   they're all
praying   sending their little
radio broadcasts up into the clouds   meanwhile
here on earth the polite and panting
hospital administrator informs me
that I'll need to take most of these flowers
home with me tonight   the bright garden
growing on your half of the room
is a fire hazard   she's very
sorry   the policies were put in place
for everyone's safety   especially that lady right
there   and she points at you
with her sausage link finger   very beautiful though
the flowers she means

The Universe Said to Invoke Infinity

how's she doing in there
the night nurse asks   she's fine I
reply   sleeping now   the nurse
turns to go   thank you for asking I say

startled she looks back   smiles and
nods   I can't stop myself from finding
her attractive which officially
makes me the most revolting human
being alive   I feel like I can't

breathe   I can't kiss you now
that I have to wear the mask   it's just a precaution
so they say

I've stopped asking every name
tagged person if you're going to be okay   I sure hope
so   that's what they say   I've come to accept

it doesn't do any good to expect
anyone to do this with me   it isn't fair
to ask them to take my share of
what they surely have too much of already

the other night when
you were sleeping   some scientist on a show about
the universe said   to invoke infinity
is the same thing as giving up   I got up and ran

to the nurse's station   I need
paper and pen   I was practically shouting   is everything
all right   they looked worried but ready
yes yes I need to write something
down   I had to write down what that man said before

I forgot his exact words   he was talking
about mathematics and the big
bang but I wanted to keep his words with me   keep them
make them mine

Preface

I can't help it   I preface
the conversations I don't want to have
with you with the phrase   the book says

as if I'm simply the minister
of more bad news   the book says
we should talk about what
you want to wear

I can't finish the sentence

I don't want to think about it   about going
through the closet   through all the clothes
I told you you didn't need   I know I'll find the
black and blue dress you wore
just once   I never understood why you kept it

new year's eve in Chicago   my god
do you remember how cold it was that year
standing outside the bar with
everyone we knew   we weren't ready
for another year   you couldn't stop
shaking   I couldn't get a cab   we were still
warm with whiskey   the pure
happiness of being young but old
enough to know it

your tears froze in black streaks on your face   no
I'm sorry   how can I possibly choose
the last thing I'll see you in

Awash

the unthinkable prospect
of a world in which I am left
to my own devices

which are few and as soon
as the batteries die useless
first order of business

I draw a map in the sand
mark where I stand as the capital
of civilization   within me the
detailed blueprints of the pyramids
and the concept of zero
beyond me the finite frontier

the many miles of undeveloped
shoreline with spectacular views of a
sea filled with intricately depicted
monsters   I have a lot to do before

I introduce the new world
to art and astronomy and industry
medicine and technology
ethics politics democracy

by a show of hands we shall elect
which tree to burn in the first fire

Crisis and Confidence

the city which had taken the whole world
was itself taken   that's what Saint
Jerome said of Rome in a letter to a friend
in the fifth century   he knew how the
world worked   he knew devastation is willing
to travel   it starts as
the part of the river you can step over   it grows

from a still source into rage and ordered force
barbarians poured through the Salarian Gate opened
fast and wide by slaves

swift as the sea
into a ship's hold   the stable world free
floating   the disaster
exactly preserved   the greatest
achievements of man crawled with men
no more than animals

no less   the noose
wound round

the throat of scholarship and law and philosophy
and politics and poverty and sickness and slavery
and corruption and decadence   history
this quickly becomes the ruins of what you thought

you built so solidly   the bronze
forms cast shadows across the lawn
of the forum   against the light
of the fire in the city
of god   my god   who didn't believe
it was too big to fall

X-Ray

there you are

a shadow caught
behind frosted glass

the doctor points to clouds
in the night sky

there   he says
and there

and there
is the airy cathedral
of ribs   the hushed
fluster of unseen
trespassers nesting in
the rafters   row after row
of empty pews
and there's you

alone before your own
dark altar   straining
to make out what's right
in front of you

The
Rhythm
of the
Empire

Lightness Arises from the Usual Gravity

we used to fight all the time
when we were younger   we're practically famous
for the night in college when we wrestled over who
knows what in the mud in someone's front
yard and rode home silently
embarrassed and visibly
drunk in the backseat of your roommate's car

we can laugh about it now
because we're here   we made it

I can tell you're thinking
about it too while the social worker slash
amateur psychologist assigned to us
by the hospital explains that it's natural
for two people like us in a time of crisis
like this to experience disagreements   we're
likely undergoing a period of extreme
distress   she's sure
she doesn't have to tell us this and I think

yes   you're right   you don't   but her endless
teleprompter turns and turns   her words
blur   she doesn't know anything
about us   I'm sure there are a hundred other
couples like us in this hospital
alone   clearly we appear to her a common
strain of the same basic devastation

that's what's hard
that's what we are

we let her finish her speech   she's been
looking at me the whole time   she must be
afraid to look at you   if she did
she'd see you're smiling
for the first time in days   when she
finally stops talking I say in all earnestness
thank you   that helps

Love and Later

luckily the trees
have the wind   it gives
them something
to do   all night the waves
batter the seawall
ceaselessly   a confusing
magnetism drives them
together   like two children
filled with a compulsion for
cruelty they'll later call
love   and later still
one of them is always
disappearing for days and
resurfacing with fistfuls
of flowers   out of habit
the other never leaves
the other says   wait
right here while I
put these in some water

Our Hour of Suspense

drowsy hours and recognition ceding
ground to sleep   I slip out past
the nurse's station   out into the night   the
parking lot practically empty   only a few lights
on at this hour in the long term wards

I know which window is yours   I know more
than I'd like to   I've memorized
the channels   we watch the shows we used to hate
the mindless waste that in days past drifted through
us in waves unnoticed   but now because we have nothing
else to do besides avoid the silence we look forward

to our hour of suspense
two partners in a police department's
sex crimes unit confront the brutality we   I mean people
are capable of   this time they're unlocking a boy
from shackles in a maniac's basement   the boy is shaking
the mother is frantic but strangely almost impossibly calm

maybe it's bad acting or maybe
I don't know how it feels to
hold the one thing you love and know the worst
is over   the show ends   the fictional boy goes on

living in the ether   we know we're supposed to be
satisfied that all is well but we also know
boys like him will never be the same

The Long Haul

like a rundown roadside diner the hospital
cafeteria is as always half filled with
newcomers   eating alone in total
silence   the uninspired fare haphazardly
arranged on hot sterile plates   soon enough
they'll come to find the pink and pale
green motif is a virus that hijacks the
appetite's machinery and shuts it down

those of us in the know venture out down the
road to the Ponderosa where the food is equally
inedible but the noise   my god   is deafening
the wonderfully obnoxious families   their
lavish celebrations of every minor occasion

No One in Particular

on the occasional and unpredictable nights
when you're without a roommate
I read aloud from whatever happens
to distract me   I read while
you drift to sleep   as I would if you were a child or
if we'd ever had one

one morning we woke early to find
we'd gotten too old for that   for a lot
of things   just a couple hundred years ago
odds are we'd both be dead by now

I read aloud *economic life was intertwined*
in these turbulent times
with the life of politics and the life of the mind
to no one in particular   there's nowhere
better than a hospital to see the only life
is the life of the body   tired I close the book and rest
my head on your chest   rises and falls
the rhythm of the empire

What Makes It Worse

what you don't know can hurt you

what you don't know can turn your body
against you

what you don't know is
why you

what are the odds of that
you don't know

twice a day and sometimes three you take a pill
to calm your anxiety over what
you don't know

a bird whose name you don't know
flies away
when you try to take its picture   where it goes
you don't know

like a child who loses sight of her mother in a crowd
what you know is separated from
what you don't

alone on the cold shore   the wind speaks
a language you've never heard before
between you and the horizon stretch the unexplored
depths of what you don't know

what makes it worse   the waves leave at your feet
all the broken pieces of what you know

The Royal Society

born from smoldering
Rome came crawling
the wretched infected
swarms   installed by hunger
behind the heavy plow they bowed
before benign and
malignant kings alike and
ate what molded bread came
their way by moon or dying
fire light   their mysterious ailments
gradually abated with equal
doses of accident and circumstance

those who lived were not yet a testament
to the inoculation of infectious agents but
rather to the faith in the impulsive
unknown who seemed to revel in choosing

you but not you
you but not you

it's a given we're not living in the dark
ages anymore but a measure of the unexplained
remains as we sit together in the examination
room while you shiver in your open
gown   the unplugged electrodes
attached to your bare back
like leeches

Romance of the Unfamiliar

mercifully our life together
hides what we can't bear
to see   our everyday depreciations

until a friend after seeing you says
Jesus man   she's wasting away
I don't know what to
call it   a relief   to hear
the clear voice of empirical truth

in my eyes you're eternally
the girl in the photo on the mantel
from the trip to Morocco   it never occurred
to me we no longer
resemble those people   it was our last day
we hadn't taken a single picture
in a week   we were too consumed
by whatever was inside us

ripening and the intrinsic romance
of the unfamiliar   our plane was leaving
in an hour   we sprinted through the
crowded streets to the mosque   I can't
remember its name   but seen through its
glass floor the breathless blue Atlantic's sun
stippled waves stunned us into
silence   taken at arm's length
you can't see any of it in the picture   nothing
other than our bright red faces

In the Wing of Catastrophe

how many weeks now
spent on innumerable floors
in the wing of catastrophe
imperceptibly the memory
of our life before has become
foreign to you as a story
you had to be there for   and as far as
you're concerned   you weren't

some days you aren't entirely sold
on having a husband   you're tired
but eventually willing
to take my word for it

other days a beautiful lucidity dwells
in you   magnificent
stretches   your body perfectly
clairvoyant channels the spirit
of your dormant self   it's nice

to see you again I say
I can tell it's you
in there because you laugh and
say   it's good to be back   is it just
me or have you gotten a little taller
since I saw you last

Emergence and Emergency

it was a simpler time then when
we were simple things   alone in the world we
performed the rote tasks of our singular
existences   once a week I walked a block

to the laundromat with my sad sack
of used clothes while you pushed a sorry cart
piled high with frozen food through the empty

aisles   we were two planes at different altitudes
on the same path   we were two trains with clueless
conductors on parallel tracks   we were sure as hell
wherever we were going we were never coming back

we weren't meant to meet but did   a party
full of someone else's friends
someone else's booze   a closet
full of someone else's clothes
and us   two sets of hands
steering reckless vehicles under the influence
of unfamiliar skin   you warned me   you said
this is going to get complicated

the future in the mirror of youth
is closer than it appears   we're here
but I still expect you to live forever   or at least
longer than me   which is the only child
of forever   I want you to know I don't
regret anything   our complexes   our love
in the face of certainty

Everything Every Time

in a different version of this I'm the one
sitting up in bed while the nurse says
deep breaths   listens to my lungs through
the cold antenna of her stethoscope   you're the one
sitting in a chair in the corner
with a half hearted smile plastered to your face

in a different version of this
we're both in bed   hunched over
while two nurses   sisters actually   listen
to our lungs   your husband and my wife
sit in the corners of the room
both of them completely useless

in a different version of this I'm in a chair
in the corner while my sister sits up
in bed   you're the nurse who listens
to my sister breathing   you glance at me for
an instant and return my uncertain smile

in a different version of this I sit up
abruptly in bed   I'm breathing deeply   you
put your hand on my back and say
go back to sleep   you're fine   everything is fine

In the
Dark
and
Wait

Pageant of Squandered Fortunes

I hate and envy almost
everyone now   I suspect their secret
happiness or can plainly see it   perfect
example   these teens on the rush hour train making
out as if the rest of the world couldn't begin
to disturb them   you can cut the disgust
in the rest of us with a knife   what a reckless
spectacle of inexpert passion   what a tactless pageant
of our squandered fortunes and the sheer dumb
luck of the young to stumble
upon it   just wait kid
one day she's got you pinned to the ground kissing
your neck and you're sure the world bends
to those whose arms are open for it   the next
she's coughing blood in the bathroom sink
a wildfire panic devours
your fields of rational thought
you drag her to the car   she begs
you to let her change her clothes and
wash her hands   they're stained
with blood   you're certain
there isn't time for that   you're certain of
almost nothing else   just wait kid   one day
you find yourself scrubbing the sink until
your fingers ache and reek of bleach but
the stain won't come out   you don't know what to do
now the thought seems plausible   just burn
the whole place to the ground

Hell Is Everyone

we enter that stretch of summer that threatens
to unhinge us   lethargic we suffer
like fish in a derelict aquarium   I sift through
the collective filth to board the train
which is the best place to join the chorus
of mutual hatred for the human race   where the
hell is everyone
going at this hour   would it kill anyone
to take a shower and what the fuck is that
guy staring at   take a picture and take a quarter
and call someone who cares
no one will answer   a woman who looks like she just
came in from the rain strains to hold up
her copy of war and peace which I could have
invented but didn't   I don't have the energy   a bead
of sweat slides down the side of her made up
face and splashes the page   the stain disappears
incrementally as she continues to read   like a time
lapse picture of a dried up sea

The Higher Order

remarkable   absolutely remarkable
the life cycles of some
parasites   the brain   the so called
crowning achievement of nature
they use it against us   for instance
the single cell beings that find
their way into rats   into their brains
their instincts   and erase
their fear of cats   in fact
the smell attracts them   it's sickening
the inefficiency of it   and hard for us
to understand   the unintentional
malice   the cat fat with its easy kill
is the final host of the last
party it will ever throw   the exposure
of the higher order cannot be
controlled   imagine the happy mice
lifted off their feet   they float
like cartoons on waves of primal
desire toward the frenzied
clenching jaws   and thus
the smallest form of life
on earth mindlessly thrives

Economies of Scale

a system reproduces
itself over space and time   you
are a system
within a system   you are a system
composed of untold
processes   within you the irreducible
particles orbit your dark
nuclear stars   within you the
ancient elements are standard
issue   but the chance array makes
you the improbable you and with
just enough variation makes
me too   but something within you
has broken down   the parts rest
unassembled on idle lines   the factory
turned to a quiet collection of precious
metals   the writing on the wall within you
the indecipherable instructions
for the world without you

Nerves

outside the flags whip ferociously

the metal clips connecting them to the ropes
clang against the pole   it's unnerving
every day they flap half mast

they do that for the soldiers one young
nurse told me   I didn't ask

you've been staring out the window
all morning   every minute since
I've been here has lived its entire life
in monastic silence and died   I want to go
outside today you say abruptly

I don't know if that's such a good idea
and I say so   but you don't care what
I don't know   and you say so

get me a fucking wheelchair if you want
just get me the fuck out of this room   I'm
suffocating in here

I hope to god it's the drugs talking   and now
you're sobbing   I'm sorry I say   I know

how you must feel   gradually the sobs subside
you close your eyes and turn away and whisper

you don't have a fucking clue how I feel

just loud enough for me to hear   before long
you're fast asleep

The Poor Souls of the Faithful

our places await us

the table still set for
a dinner delayed by months
of negative tests   by guess
after educated guess   our kitchen
is the picture of an abandoned
town   the mysterious inhabitants
up and left   here is the still life

of what they've lost   the sad remains
of a landscape drained
of all it was worth   the plates

collect a fine dust and the wine
glasses too   I can't say
what makes me afraid
to disturb them   the way some families
leave a space for the one departed

here we're both ghosts
we who eat in silence but not before

we thank the lord for this
generous feast   this gift
of insatiable craving we've so
graciously taken   he who won't
take it back   he who has given us
what he wants us to believe
we deserve   he who asks us to ration
our already diminishing portions

Vital

we're superfluous organs
in the sickly sweet cavity of the medical
beast   they've clearly forgotten
we're in here and why not   we're not
vital for the thing to live   it breathes and feeds
and sleeps with us inside   it stretches its ambulatory legs
and yawns as only those animals do who
fear nothing   you're burning alive   you're cold
and swollen   becoming a real bother it seems   to tell
the truth   the half life of compassion
is days   the night's bright filament fizzles   decays
lightning between wires the synapses fire
announcing pain   the great beast winces and begins
to moan in its sleep

Because It Feeds Us

it tears away the succulent center
and tosses the charred parts
at our feet   eat
it says   and we eat

because it feeds us   it takes
a swig of wine which drips
in ribbons
down its chin
onto a shirt

stained already
with grease and the juices
of other suffering

it wants
to know if we'd like
something to drink and we do

which makes the whole
cavern of its stomach quake

which frightens the
shrieking bats of its laughter
out of slumber

it spits on the floor

drink   it says   till
you've had your fill

Another Instance in Which I'm Good for Nothing

for a while I was convinced
you were in love

with your doctor   how could
I blame you   there he was

doing everything
in his power to save your life

and here I am   holding
a bag full of batteries

and not a single one
the size you need

Base Pairs

at night I feel it more acutely   the information
passing through me
from one device to another leaves traces
in my cell walls like holes
where former occupants of a place once hung
their secondhand frames   I feel them
streaming through me   the words of two young lovers
whose every day ends
with the one repeated promise they fully intend to keep
god love them
their shorthand sequence decodes love's genome
believe me I try but I can't understand it
to know that someone does will have to be enough

Acceptance

it's a beautiful thought after
all   to think   with just the right
sense of distance   we're nearly
nonexistent   that the fingers we use
to count the people who love us
unconditionally will slowly
fold into a fist in which we've
caught a drowsy firefly   when
we let it go   a long moment passes
in which it's lost in the night sky
unconsciously we hold
our breath in the dark and wait

To the Prospects of the Experimental

the rate of positive response
in infected mice is promising

he goes on

somewhere in the neighborhood
of seventy five percent

is that good I ask

oh yes he says   what we call
statistically significant

you don't say anything

you're picturing a trash can
filled to the brim with one hundred
percent dead mice

here we are   clinging to the root
of promising   to the prospects of the
experimental   the hope inherent

you're not a rat exactly   but that's
okay it seems   they're more interested
in humans now   before he leaves

he pats your shoulder gently   as if
you were an orphan in an old movie
and this kind fellow just opened the door
to the room you'll be sharing
with the rest of them

no need to thank me
his smile says   you thank him anyway

let's keep those fingers crossed
he says   okay

okay

Tepid

I still can't bring myself to watch
them stick the needle in your back   you put up little
resistance   a switch
is flipped   you become the tortured
trunk of a wind ravaged tree   rigid above an obsidian
swamp of pain   mosquitoes linger
at the surface   you feel them all over
little diligent syringes drawing blood until
they decide enough is
enough   the muscles constrict   hard
as bark   ashen limbs host a murder of birds
prematurely dressed for mourning   your mouth a hollow
O   inside the restless snake
uncoils in the humidity of its new fangled hunger

They Run You

to get the horse to do
what you want it to do
you practically have to
kill it first   I guess
that's what they're
doing to you   they
want your body to
respond the way their
manual says it should
they run you
ragged   all day long
until the dust coats
your lungs   until you wheeze
when you try to breathe
and your iron black eyes
stare off into a distance
you're sure
you don't have the heart
to go   you can feel
everything inside you
breaking   come on
girl   faster   yeah
that's it   faster

Deep into the Treatments

every minute of every day is like the morning
after a spectacular party
that everyone in attendance can only remember
up to a certain point

for instance
when Matt told everyone he was seeing his
ex again and he
seemed genuinely happy which he hasn't been
for as long as anyone can recall including
when he was married to her and

after that it was simply a blur
like it was when we were children   when people still
drove places for quote unquote vacations
and we were too small to see
squarely out the window so we angled our heads back
against the seats and watched the green ruffled sheet of trees
flap across the sky until we fell asleep

you awoke decades later in this room
and now everything that seemed to make you so happy
makes you want to be sick

Apollo the Healer

the idea is the ideal
a young man
in the sunlight
of his days
a good boy
falls out of the tree
but doesn't fall
far   he's an apple
in the grass   his red
delicious skin   the sun
reaches down through the
clouds as he drifts
to sleep   the sun runs
its fingers down the length
of his thigh and sighs
but lingers too long
the earth begins to burn
everyone wants to be
the sun except the sun

In a Sedimental Mood

let go of me   you say as calmly
as you can   I'm not a baby

you're right   the way you shuffle
along the side of the wide
hospital hallway has a glacial intensity

a learned determination culled from years
of scale model devastations   the uninitiated
babies of the world rush
headlong into every small accomplishment
their little animal hands outstretched
to catch their balance in the spinning dizzy

unreachable now   but you you're not
a baby   you know exactly
where you're going and the godless world
will have to strike you dead to keep you
from reaching the end of it

Disproving the Humors

in the morning I arrive to find you
sprawled across the bed   your left leg dangling
your arms limp at your sides and your eyes
wide open   tongue lolling

I stand over you for a moment and
wait for you to blink   you're hilarious
I say but nothing moves   my pulse quickens
the gullible instincts   come on
I say   that's enough   blink

but you don't   as soon as I move my shaking
fingers toward your neck a young man arrives
with breakfast and you rise from the dead
and say are you kidding me   pancakes again

Belongings

years ago in Mexico we saw a church
built in the fifteenth century   the bus didn't stop
we were on our way to something
more important and the guide had simply pointed
as we passed   this church he said was constructed
by the Spanish with the stones of a Mayan temple
razed to ruins by the Spanish   he said the word
Spanish twice with emphasis   then
twice more when he translated what he'd said
into Spanish   Español   unable to pull apart
the speaker from the spoken   whatever happened
to the Mayans a little girl asked from the back and
our guide produced a series of halting guttural sounds
then paused for effect   that is the Mayan way he said
to say   we are alive   we are everywhere

I stand transfixed holding a box of our things
that were supposed to make you feel more
at home   a couple framed photos   a glass owl
that belonged to your mother   a small ceramic skull
rests on top   tourist junk sure but you loved
the way the painted teeth seemed to smile

through the window I see you squirming
in the idling car in the parking lot below   turning
the various dials one way then another
like some kind of out of work astronaut

a cleaning woman I don't recognize enters
the room and says excuse me and slips past
to change the sheets for the bed's next resident

Back
to
You

The Renaissance

you wake to the sunbeams forming
acute angles through the shadeless window

the faithful chapel of distance looms
in the square where you return to your labors

so close to heaven
the faces you paint drip lovingly back to you

another day is all but over
you've forgotten to eat lunch again   the sudden hunger
a stumbled upon underground river

you tell the waitress you'll have the usual and she looks
embarrassed with her hands full
of pen and paper   she stares hard at the empty table

it doesn't matter you've been here
a million times   she doesn't know what you want

Get Used to It

suddenly no one wonders
how your pain is today
on a scale of one to ten   it's your first
day home and something feels not
just different but
wrong   I killed the plant you kept
from your mother's funeral   there's a halo
of crust on the table from the water
it wouldn't hold   it was too much
it was too late   I'm sorry

but no you say   that's not it
though you're not too happy about that either
it's something harder to name

just knowing I've been living in these rooms
without you for what seems like forever
maybe you think I've learned
how to get used to it

the idea of forever

By Now

asleep your fingers twitch
in syncopated rhythm
to a dream   flex and
relax   they grasp at
something I can't
see   something you can't
quite hold   it kills me
to know this is only
one of a million things
I never noticed
when I loved you too
easily   when time was a
glass of water the waiter
refilled without even
asking me   I was too busy
with sleep to see you
had already boarded
the train that was taking
you away   one hand waving
the other reaching for
what I was already too far
away by now to see

The History of Right Now

the sun burns away
the morning fog   there it is

the miracle of the city   there's me and
there's you   miracles in our own right   coming up

with our own reasons for being here
our best excuses   the sun too

I almost forgot

another miracle   so many of them they
start to seem ordinary   inevitable   as if there were nothing
miraculous about anything anymore

I refuse to believe it
for instance the man with a bent leg who gives up
his seat on the bus for

the tired woman towing
a little child behind her and inside her
another waiting

I can barely take it   I can hardly breathe thinking
about the millions of years it took

to turn the ancient world's plants and animals
into a thick black serum and the first
century Chinese who found it with their bamboo poles
and the thousands of years it took to refine
the process of extracting it out of the ground

and Samuel Brown who adapted
the steam engine to burn the fuel and Gottlieb Daimler
and Karl Benz who made it practical and

here we are now   barreling up combustible Broadway
making all the stops and all the while this child
clings to his mother's hand   out of the blue

he'll produce sounds that his mother
and everyone can understand

here and there her words too will breach the surface
of his consciousness   without even trying
he'll become one of us   and his little brother or

sister too   curled in the amniotic bliss   churning
those tiny legs   the incredible little pistons pumping

Given Everything

the first days of your life
restored and you hardly want
to leave the house   in your mind you're still
a fugitive to disease   your hands and face
stained with the dark ink of illicit
fortune   so many remaining
days stacked in neat piles before you
on the kitchen table   more time
than you've ever laid eyes on and nowhere
to spend it   your paranoid heart cowers
in your chest   days pass in the disbelief of this
difficult freedom   you find you want so little
given everything

A Good Year

dead tired from the unremarkable splendor
of a summer Sunday spent
living unencumbered under the sun from

which we're turning now
helplessly away   our thoughts
wander without conviction and crumple

into patio chairs   the night sky
bright with stadium lights   sporadic cheers rise
erratic above the crackling

radio's persistent murmur   it occurs to me
these must have always been
our best days   but the details bleed into the ether
the hollow spaces that separate the manic else

though we will
let's say we'll never forget the song
was Louis Jordan's is you is or is you ain't my baby

and that night Starlin Castro hit a stand up triple
to drive in the winning run in the middle of
another futile season

we were beginning to see he might be just like
the rest of us   he had a good year that year but
maybe that's as good as he'd ever be

Disgrace

one time
when things were bad and only
getting worse I
told you I was working
late and even though
your voice on the other end
breathless and beaten said

oh god   you can't   I need
to see you now   please
I'm begging   please

I said with coldblooded
composure   sorry   there's
nothing I can do about it

and hung up and drove
right past the hospital
to the megaplex   it was
almost empty that time
of day   what's the least
popular movie you've got
I asked the girl inside the glass cage
and she told me and I took
my ticket and gave it to the boy
who tore it in half and gave it
back to me   right then

I was convinced
you were going to die
while I sat in the back
of that goddamn theater
I wanted so bad to have
to myself

You're Supposed to Laugh

a nun sits outside the church
naked and smoking
the priest comes up and says
what in god's name is going on here
sorry the nun says
dirty habit

I watch your face for signs
of life   nothing
not even a smirk

once a registered sucker
for Catholic humor
since the illness you're impervious
to any emotion
closely associated with joy

you're supposed to laugh I say
remember laughter

evidently you do not
or you're still thinking about it
or you'd like me to
shut the fuck up and leave
you alone   which is all
you've said all day

an ad for a new reality show ends
the ten o'clock news resumes

the man singing the blues resumes
the animals boarding the leaky boat
in twos resumes
the woman who came to believe
she had nothing left to lose resumes

and how should she resume
and how should she begin

Physical Therapy

please   you say   don't look at me
I'm disgusting   emaciated
by the treatments   you swear
they gave you the wrong
body to bring home   here's something
you'd like to know   who
is this woman wearing your clothes

they don't even fit her   look at her
she's a complete mess   lays in bed all day
it's pathetic   get up   you scream
at her   get up   come on I say   that's enough
she needs to rest

bullshit you say and grab her arm   pull
her to her feet   walk   you demand
but she can't   you shove her
a little too hard   she pitches forward
like a wave toward the shore
and shatters across the floor

now look what you've done

carefully I piece her back together
from memory

You're Welcome

now that you're not dying
faster than the rest of us you want
to spend every waking
hour outside in the very same
kind of garden you once described
as the biggest waste of time and energy
our idiot hippie neighbors ever devised

I don't say a word

now you're down in the dirt all day
creating and sustaining
life until the evening breeze blows
right through your blousy skin and rattles your
fragile skeleton   until you can barely stand
it   slowly I help you
out of your clothes
ragged and dirty and into a bath

rest now   let the water
bring you back   I'll
be waiting for you   I'll
be in the kitchen slicing the tomatoes you made
for a lousy dinner that will
nonetheless reduce you to tears and cause
you to thank me profusely

As Soon as We're Outside

I realize now how badly we missed
the point   how stupid we were

to keep a record of only what we thought
to be extraordinary   mountain peaks
bisected by thin clouds   the crystal clear
water that washes the shores of the world's
leaked secrets   the lazy
harbors   the darkness under the canopies
of corrugated roofs that funnel torrents of rain
into rusted buckets   as soon as we're outside
ourselves the ordinary becomes exotic

there's almost no evidence
we existed there besides the implicit
witness of our pictures   when present we're
never together   there's me standing alone before
some beautiful enormity   and there's you
in the center of all

the bewildered children   their mouths gaping and
glistening as if filled with inconceivable
snow   they'd never seen anything like you before
I remember when I first knew exactly how they felt

Swell

we become accustomed to the temperate
climate of our contentment   our cloudless gratitude
a flawless blue over the swell
of traffic in the evening   the gradual retreat

of the day's exhausted heat
the sound an uncanny echo of waves   bright against
the muted sky the birds return
from a distant winter to feast on a harvest of insects

Notes

"On Airs Waters and Places"
The poem shares its title with a treatise from the Hippocratic Corpus, a collection of ancient Greek medical texts, of which the Hippocratic Oath is one.

"No One in Particular"
The italicized lines are borrowed from Emma Rothschild's *Economic Sentiments: Adam Smith, Condorcet, and the Enlightenment* (Harvard University Press, 2001).

Acknowledgments

I'm incredibly thankful to the editors of the journals where some of these poems first appeared: *Bat City Review, Catch Up,* the *Cincinnati Review, Cobalt Review, Green Mountains Review, Pebble Lake Review, Verse Daily,* and *Zone 3.*

Thank you, Tom Sleigh, for selecting this book and changing my life. Thank you, too, for your kindness and insight. Thank you to Michael Collier and everyone at Bread Loaf. I'm indebted to Jeff Shotts for his keen vision that improved every poem in this book. An infinite number of thanks to Fiona McCrae and everyone at Graywolf for giving my book a beautiful home and for making me feel a part of the pack.

I could never thank enough those who have encouraged and inspired me: Mark Doty, Tony Hoagland, Kimiko Hahn, James Reiss, Claudia Rankine, Glenn Shaheen, Brian Nicolet, Christopher Munde, Paul Otremba, Kent Shaw, Hannah Gamble, Sophie Rosenblum, and Andrew Brininstool. Thanks to the Inprint Foundation and the University of Houston Creative Writing Program for bringing so many great writers together. Special thanks to Christopher Ankney, whose genius is everywhere to be found in here.

To Linda Wallenberg, who started all of this.

To my family, who have always been my biggest fans.

To my beautiful wife, Stephanie—this is for you.

Brian Russell earned an MFA from the University of Houston, where he served as poetry editor for *Gulf Coast.* His poems have appeared in *Bat City Review,* the *Cincinnati Review, Epoch, Mid-American Review,* and *Verse Daily.* He lives with his wife and dogs in Chicago.

Bread Loaf and the Bakeless Prizes

The Katharine Bakeless Nason Literary Publication Prizes were established in 1995 to expand the Bread Loaf Writers' Conference's commitment to the support of emerging writers. Endowed by the LZ Francis Foundation, the prizes commemorate Middlebury College patron Katharine Bakeless Nason and launch the publication career of a poet, a fiction writer, and a creative nonfiction writer annually. Winning manuscripts are chosen in an open national competition by a distinguished judge in each genre. Winners are published by Graywolf Press.

2012 Judges

Tom Sleigh
Poetry

Randall Kenan
Fiction

The text of *The Year of What Now* is set in Centaur, a typeface originally designed by Bruce Rogers for the Metropolitan Museum in 1914 and modeled on letters cut by the fifteenth-century printer Nicolas Jenson. Book design by Ann Sudmeier. Composition by BookMobile Design and Digital Publisher Services, Minneapolis, Minnesota. Manufactured by Versa Press on acid-free, 30 percent postconsumer wastepaper.